National Historic Landmarks
of
ALASKA
COLORING BOOK

978-1-73-712823-6

Welcome to the National Historic Landmarks of Alaska Coloring Book

Coloring books are beloved for their many benefits: reducing stress, improving hand-eye coordination, gaining clarity, increasing self-confidence, and the simple joy of bringing a piece of artwork to life. There are few barriers to coloring pages and they can be taken anywhere. There's no better way for kids and adults to relax and learn about Alaska's role in U.S. history than coloring their way through 14,000 years of some of Alaska's most important places.

The following pages offer many of Alaska's National Historic Landmarks in illustrations that express the architecture, family, community, commerce, joys, tragedies, action, and new connections that make these landmarks so special. National Historic Landmarks are places that are important to the history of the United States. Their listing in the National Register of Historic Places is a recognition that they are exceptional. Alaska is home to 50 National Historic Landmarks and over 420 National Register of Historic Places properties. These special places are integral to some of our nation's most important stories of conflict, achievement, and cultural lineage over tens of thousands of years to the modern era.

With the vignettes of history presented in the National Historic Landmarks in Alaska Coloring Book we hope to inspire curiosity and creativity in people of all ages and from all walks of life. You can print the entire coloring book or print single pages of the landmarks that spark your interest. Share them with your classroom, co-workers, family, and friends.

This coloring book was developed by the National Park Service, Interior Region 11 – Alaska, National Historic Landmark Program. We worked with local Alaska science illustrator Kristin Link who reviewed contemporary and historic images for inspiration in creating the illustrations. Furthermore, we sought the advice of community members who have close ties to the history of these National Historic Landmarks, cultural specialists, and linguists to incorporate their personal and academic knowledge creating this celebratory and educational book.

Sincerely,
Heritage Assistance Program
(Janet Clemens, Rhea Hood,
Erik Johnson, and John Wachtel)
Interior Region 11 - Alaska
National Park Service

Learn more about the National Historic Landmarks in this book
WWW.NPS.GOV/SUBJECTS/NHLALASKA

Acknowledgments & Sources

We would especially like to acknowledge these individuals and organizations with our sincerest gratitude for their contributions:

Vernae Agnaboogok, Richard Atuk, Robert Tokienna, and the Wales Tribal Council

Alaska Department of Fish and Game

Darling Anderson, Moses Dirks, Mike Livingston, and the Aleutian Pribilof Islands Association

Joanne Bryant, Gwich'in Language Interpretation and Translation

Karen Evanoff and Lake Clark National Park and Preserve

Gates of the Arctic National Park and Preserve

Iñupiat Heritage and Language Center

Klondike Gold Rush National Historical Park

Kobuk Valley National Park

Heidi Kritz, Bristol Bay Native Association, and the Qayassiq Walrus Commission

U.S. Fish and Wildlife Service

Visiting National Historic Landmarks

If you would like to visit Alaska's National Historic Landmarks in person, please check ahead of time about ownership status and any requirements. While some NHLs are managed by the National Park Service (NPS), most NHL properties are privately owned, and others are managed by non-profit organizations, state, and other federal agencies.

We support public and private efforts to identify, evaluate, and protect America's historic and archeological resources. If you know of a property that's important to the history of your community, we can provide guidance on nomination for the National Register of Historic Places and help qualified property owners apply for preservation benefits and incentives.

Learn more about nominating your property to the National Register of Historic Places through the Alaska Office of History & Archaeology, the Alaska Region NPS office, or the Washington D.C. headquarters for the National Register of Historic Places program.

National Historic Landmarks in Alaska

1. Attu Battlefield & US Army and Navy Airfields on Attu
2. Japanese Occupation Site, Kiska Island
3. Adak Army Base & Adak Naval Operating Base
4. Anangula Archeological District
5. Chaluka Site
6. Fort Glenn, Umnak Island
7. Dutch Harbor Naval Operating Base & Fort Mears, US Army
8. Church of the Holy Ascension
9. Sitka Spruce Plantation
10. Seal Islands Historic District
11. Walrus Islands Archeological District
12. Brooks River Archeological District
13. Amalik Bay Archeological District
14. Three Saints Bay
15. Kodiak Naval Operating Base & Forts Greely and Abercrombie
16. Russian-American Company Magazin
17. Kijik Archeological District
18. Yukon Island Main Site
19. Church of the Assumption of the Virgin Mary (Holy Assumption Orthodox Church)
20. Palugvik Archeological District
21. Bering Expedition Landing Site
22. New Russia Site
23. Chilkoot Trail & Dyea Site
24. Skagway Historic District & White Pass
25. Fort William H. Seward
26. Fort Durham Site
27. Kake Cannery
28. Alaska Native Brotherhood Hall
29. American Flag Raising Site
30. Russian-American Building No. 29
31. St. Michael's Cathedral
32. Old Sitka
33. Russian Bishop's House
34. Sheldon Jackson School
35. Sitka Naval Operating Base & US Army Coastal Defenses
36. Kennecott Mines
37. Dry Creek Archeological Site
38. Ladd Field
39. SS Nenana (River Steamboat)
40. George C. Thomas Memorial Library
41. Eagle Historic District
42. Iyatayet Site
43. Cape Nome Mining District and Discovery Sites
44. Wales Sites
45. Cape Krusenstern Archeological District
46. Ipiutak Site
47. Onion Portage Archeological District
48. Gallagher Flint Station Archeological Site
49. Leffingwell Camp Site
50. Birnirk Site

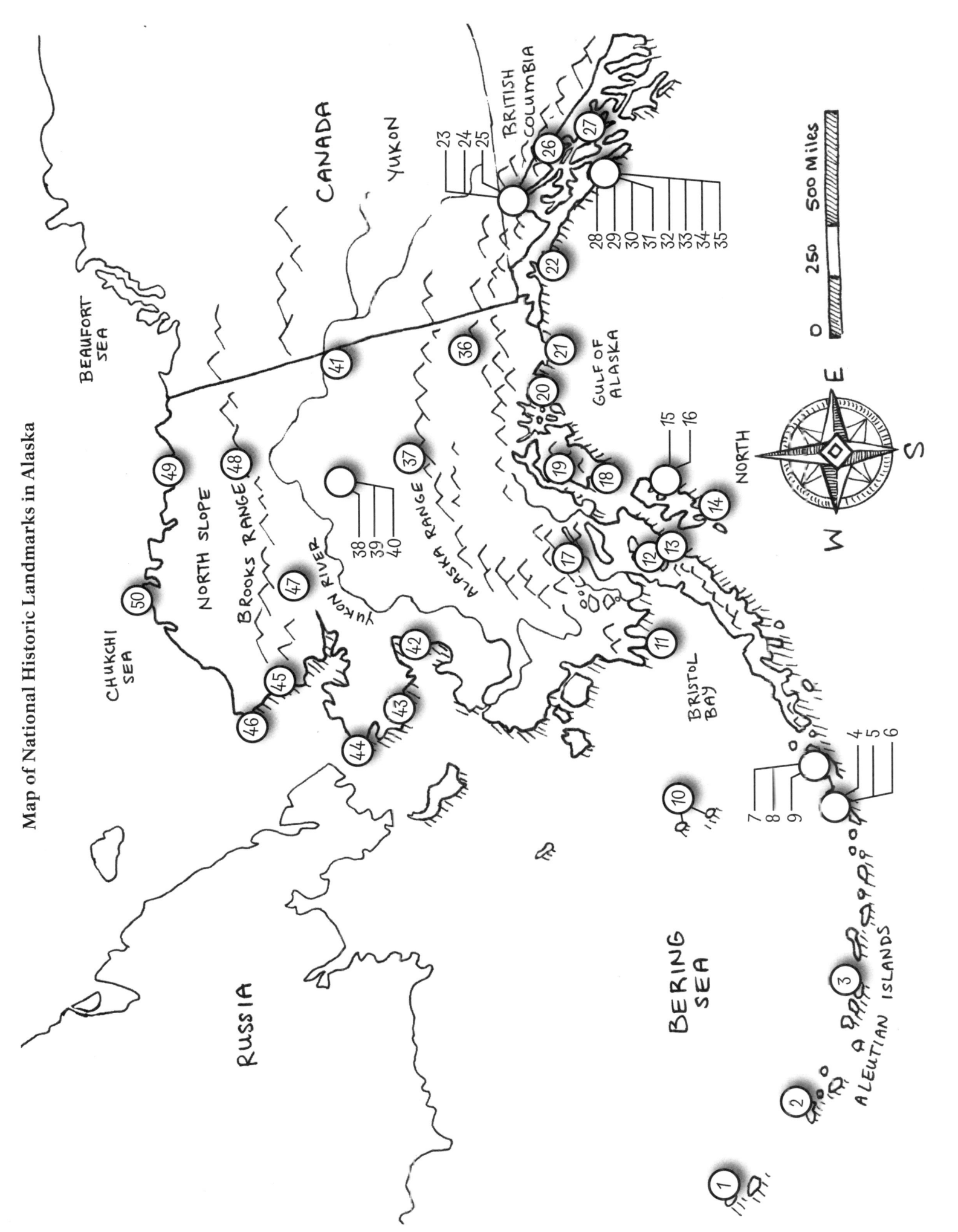

Map of National Historic Landmarks in Alaska

Alaska Native Brotherhood Hall National Historic Landmark
Sitka, Alaska

Alaska Native Brotherhood (ANB), Sitka Camp No. 1, is the original chapter of local camps in Alaska and the Pacific Northwest. Founded in 1912, the ANB developed out of the efforts of Tlingit communities to fight bans against Alaska Natives in restaurants and movie theaters. For the first half of the 20th century the Alaska Native Brotherhood (with the Alaska Native Sisterhood founded in 1915) was the only organization representing the interests of Alaska Natives. ANB was instrumental in gaining full U.S. citizenship for Alaska Natives in 1924, and with fighting racial segregation practices that resulted in the Alaska legislature passing the first anti-discrimination law in the nation in 1946. Today, the Alaska Native Brotherhood/Sisterhood camps are an important force in preserving indigenous heritage. The Sitka ANB Hall continues to serve the community as a camp headquarters and is available to the public for social events and community activities.

Walrus Islands Archeological District National Historic Landmark
Bristol Bay, Alaska

Bristol Bay people have been visiting the islands since at least 4300 BCE (Before Common Era), and archeological evidence shows that people have been hunting walrus there for at least the past 6,000 years. Harvesting walrus is a tradition for many arctic and subarctic communities in Greenland, Russia, Canada, and Alaska. Alaska Native Yup'ik, Iñupiaq and Unangax̂ communities continue to depend on walrus. The Walrus Islands are made up of seven small islands – Qayassiq ("place to go in a kayak" or Round Island), Qilkeq (named after a person in a legend or Summit Island), Nunalukaq ("land big enough to live on awhile" or Crooked Island), Ingriqvak ("big island" or High Island), Ingricuar ("small island" or Black Rock Island), and Nunevragak ("temporary camping place" or The Twins islands).

**Adak Army Base and Adak Naval Operating Base National Historic Landmark
Adak Island, Alaska**

Adak Army and Navy operating bases provided significant support for WWII U.S. military efforts to retake Attu and Kiska, the western most Aleutian Islands. Built in response to the Japanese invasion and occupation, Adak's airfield provided proximity to the islands, which allowed fighter plane protection of the bombers to intensifying bombing of the Japanese garrisons. Ships and submarines of the North Pacific Force aided in the fight against the enemy in northern waters. As combat soldiers amassed on Adak in preparation for retaking Kiska, the island's rugged tundra-covered terrain and fierce weather provided ideal conditions for training the Allied amphibious invasion force. Military personnel lived in canvas tents and Quonset huts and made the most of their recreational time including playing baseball (Illustration inspired by a 1943 photograph taken by a soldier serving on Adak and Kiska, NPS Sam Maloof WWII in Alaska Photograph Collection).

Bering Expedition Landing Site National Historic Landmark
Kayak Island, Alaska

The 1741 Bering Expedition landing at Kayak Island in the Gulf of Alaska is considered by many as the first scientific investigation of Northwestern North America. Georg W. Steller, a surgeon and naturalist, accompanied Vitus Bering on the Russian sent Great Northern Expedition. Steller spent 10 hours on the island - the first documented attempt at contact between Europeans and Alaska's Native people. While the explorers saw no people, there were dwellings in the area and obvious signs of recent human activity. Steller's journal entries, and his collections of natural specimens and cultural items, provided knowledge of the natural and human history of this area of the world to the explorers. While his collection of cultural items from around the landing site was the first of such collections from Alaska it is also an example of the European colonial practice of taking various belongings of indigenous peoples without their consent.

Skagway Historic District and White Pass National Historic Landmark
Skagway, Alaska

Beginning in Skagway, the White Pass Trail opened in 1897 and became a major transportation route for thousands of gold seekers enroute to the Yukon. By 1898, the Klondike Gold Rush had transformed Skagway from a homestead at the foot of a pioneer pack trail to a city of 10,000. By 1910, the population of Skagway had diminished to 872. Today the remaining buildings of the once booming gold rush city serve as the physical embodiment of the Gold Rush Era. Historic buildings include shops, saloons, a train depot, homes, and cabins. The Moore homestead illustrated in the drawing above tells the story of triumphs and tragedies faced by many dealing with a rapidly changing society. The National Park Service offers tours of the Moore Homestead and many other Gold Rush Era buildings at Klondike Gold Rush National Historical Park in Skagway.

**Ladd Field National Historic Landmark
Fort Wainwright, Alaska**

American and Soviet pilots met at Ladd Field when the U.S. transferred aircraft to the Soviet Union as part of the Lend-Lease Program during World War II. Ladd Field, near Fairbanks, played a crucial role as the transfer point of nearly 8,000 aircraft for use on the European front. Construction of Ladd Field began in August 1939 and went into operation in September 1940. It was the first U.S. Army airfield in Alaska and a part of the defense build-up for the war. Ladd Field was the Alaskan headquarters for the Alaska-Siberia Lend-Lease route. The military post is also significant for development of cold weather aviation technology, and for the supporting role it played in the Aleutian Campaign of World War II in the Pacific. Today, Ladd Field is within the boundaries of the Fort Wainwright Army base (Illustration inspired by photographs from UAF and Pioneer Museum).

Russian Bishop's House National Historic Landmark
Sitka, Alaska

The Russian Bishop's House was the residence of Ivan Veniaminov (also known as Rev. Ioann Veniaminov, and later canonized as Saint Innocent of Alaska), the first Bishop of Alaska. Located in Sitka and built from 1841-1843, it served as the administrative center for the Bishop and other Orthodox missionary efforts among Alaska's indigenous people. This influence can still be observed today, with numerous Orthodox communicants living in the Aleutian and Pribilof Islands, and other Alaskan coastal communities. The building itself is significant from an architectural and engineering point of view due to its unique construction characteristics of Russian vernacular design, including intricate joinery methods, and a more sophisticated building system for distributing loads than that typically found in log construction on this continent. Today, the National Park Service offers guided tours of the building, which has been restored to its 1853 appearance.

Saint Michael's Cathedral National Historic Landmark
Sitka, Alaska

The Cathedral of St. Michael of the Archangel (commonly known as St. Michael's Cathedral) is located in the center of the business district of Sitka, Alaska, the town which was the capital of Russian America from 1808 to 1867. The original structure was built between 1844 and 1848 and would experience relatively little modification or renovation for the next 118 years until a catastrophic fire in 1966 burned it to the ground. While the building was completely lost, many of the icons, royal doors and chandelier were saved. Thanks to measurements taken in 1942 and subsequent drawings completed in 1961 as part of a Historic American Buildings Survey (HABS) project, the building was faithfully reconstructed using more fire-resistant materials from 1967-76.

Birnirk National Historic Landmark
Utqiagvik, Alaska

The Birnirk National Historic Landmark (known locally as Piġniq) sits on the Chukchi Sea coast in the town of Utqiagvik, Alaska. The Birnirk archeological tradition is the earliest instance of Iñupiat culture in northern Alaska. This tradition lasted from about 500 CE to 900 CE (Common Era). The technology that developed at this site (and other Birnirk sites) supported population expansion across the arctic regions of North America and Greenland. Piġniq is Iñupiaq for 'joint' and describes the lagoon of the archeological district. The landmark is made up of a series of mounds on beach ridges. The mounds reach up to 14-feet tall and are dimpled with the sunken remains of house ruins and cache pits. Today, the National Historic Landmark remains a popular area for duck hunting.

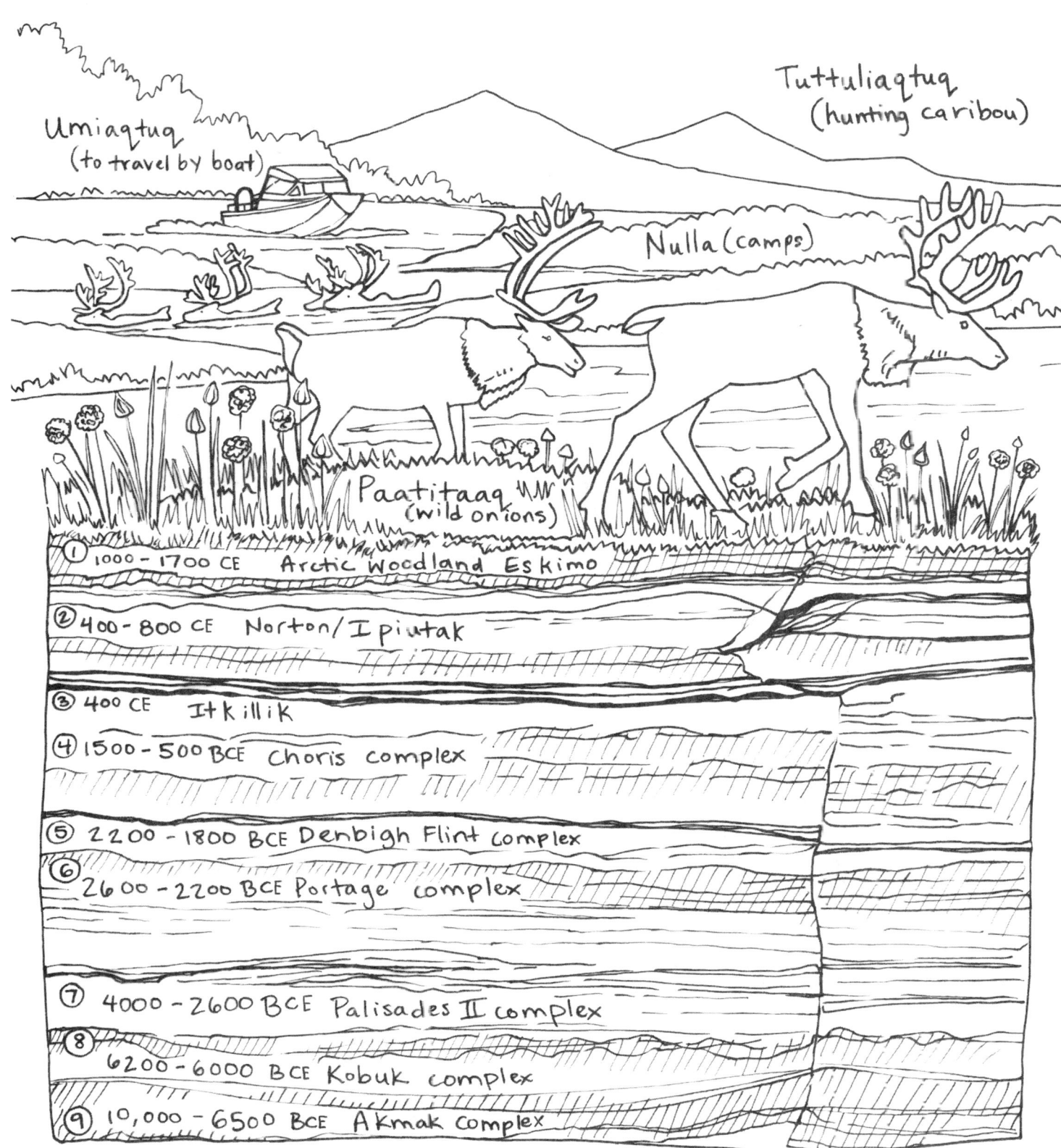

Onion Portage Archeological District National Historic Landmark
Kobuk Valley, Alaska

Onion Portage, known locally as Paatitaaq, is roughly 100 miles east of the mouth of the Kobuk River and has been occupied for at least the last 8,000 years. Paatitaaq (Iñupiaq for "wild onions") is known by archeologists for its many layers of stratigraphy with the remains of thousands of years of camping, hunting, tool manufacturing, preparing game, and building homes at Onion Portage and surrounding area. Today, communities in the Kobuk River Valley continue to rely on fishing, hunting, and gathering as an important component of their local economy. When the Western Arctic caribou herd crosses the Kobuk River during its biannual migrations, locals continue the thousands of years of hunting traditions at Onion Portage.

Kennecott Mines National Historic Landmark
Kennecott, Alaska

Located in Wrangell-St. Elias National Park and Preserve, the Kennecott Mines were once among the nation's largest, and contained the last of the great high-grade copper ore deposits discovered in the American West. By designing the world's first ammonia-leaching plant at the remote site, the Kennecott Copper Corporation was able to extract higher concentrates of ore from the low-grade ores which were once disregarded. The site includes the mill town with its dominating fourteen-story wood frame mill building, system of tramways, and camps at the Bonanza, Glacier, Jumbo, and Erie mines. Mining operations occurred between 1901 and 1938, after which many of the buildings, structures and artifacts were abandoned in situ. The National Park Service acquired many of the significant buildings and lands of the historic mining town in 1998 and have since worked to preserve the historic integrity of the mill town for future generations.

Russian-American Company Magazin National Historic Landmark
Kodiak, Alaska

The Russian-American Company Magazin is the oldest of only four Russian structures standing in the U.S and is the only surviving structure known to have been associated with both the Russian-American Company and the Alaska Commercial Company. Likely built in 1808, the Magazin (or storehouse) was built of traditional Russian horizontal log construction. The building was used as a warehouse for furs collected by the Russian-American Company, primarily seal and sea otter, but also beaver, fox, bear, lynx, sable mink and wolverine. As ownership changed over the years, so too did the building's purpose. The building has experienced modifications to accommodate a more residential use, including a gable roof and other additions to the original log structure. Today, the Magazin serves as the Kodiak History Museum.

Sitka Spruce Plantation National Historic Landmark
Unalaska, Alaska

The Aleutian Islands are remarkable for their treeless landscapes with far-off views of tundra valleys, snowcapped mountain peaks, steaming volcano tops, and the deep blue Pacific Ocean. In 1805 a Russian colony had settled on Unalaska. Desiring to be as self-sufficient as possible, they planted spruce trees imported from Southeast Alaska. Here on Amaknak Island, is the first recorded afforestation (planting trees where none had grown before) project on the North America continent. The fierce Aleutian winds, however, prevented trees from growing tall. By 1975, only six of the original Sitka spruce were still growing but hundreds of small saplings surrounded them. Today these trees are enjoyed as part of Unalaska's Sitka Spruce Park. Walking along a trail that winds through the remains of the plantation gives one the feeling of being in a forest, a rare experience in the Aleutians.

George C. Thomas Memorial Library National Historic Landmark
Fairbanks, Alaska

The George C. Thomas Memorial Library was an important community space in the early history of Fairbanks. The town was founded after a gold rush arrived in 1902, and not long after, Episcopal missionaries saw the need to provide reading materials to the isolated population. Since its construction in 1909, the building has mostly functioned as a library for Fairbanks with other significant meetings occurring there. In 1915, the library was host to a historic meeting between Alaska Territory officials and a group of Tanana Chiefs, where they discussed land claims, employment and educational opportunities. The meeting marked one of the earliest organized efforts by Alaska Natives to receive compensation for their lands. The building is named for a major donor who never visited Alaska. It is now privately owned.

Sheldon Jackson School National Historic Landmark
Sitka, Alaska

The history of Sheldon Jackson School begins with the arrival of Presbyterian missionaries ten years after the 1867 purchase of Alaska from Russia. Reverend Sheldon Jackson was one of the first to recruit fellow missionaries for work in Alaska. Jackson was appointed General Agent of Education for Alaska, following passage of the federal Organic Act of 1884 that provided for civil government and public education. Through education that emphasized English, students were taught to adopt elements of Euro-American culture. Changes in Alaska Native life were also instigated by the removal of native students from their homes to the school, and by the promotion of skills other than those used in traditional Native occupations. The school also played an important although indirect role, through its students, in the development of Alaska Native political organization and the pursuit of legal rights.

Japanese Occupation Site National Historic Landmark
Kiska Island, Alaska

Japanese troops occupied Kiska for over fourteen months during WWII. They developed a base by digging in, creating sod walls to protect structures, as well as building underground tunnels, air raid shelters and hospitals. Anti-aircraft guns and coastal defense guns were strategically placed to counter air attacks and potential naval invasion. Following the loss of Attu, Japanese command realized their precarious position. In late July 1943, Japanese ships evacuated troops under fog cover and sailed away undetected. They left their base with naval wreckage after a year of intense bombings by the Allies. The joint American and Canadian forces arrived, unaware of the vacated island, and sustained casualties by friendly fire and landmines. They established camps, developed the runway and dock area; the Aleutian Campaign was over. Today's battlefield landscape reflects a remarkable degree of the Japanese and Allied occupations, with no other development on the island having taken place.

Wales Sites National Historic Landmark
Kiŋigin, Wales, Alaska

The Wales Sites National Historic Landmark is made up of the Kurigitavik Mound site and the Hillside site. These archeological sites date back to at least 500 CE (Common Era) and include artifacts from the Birnirk archeological culture (the earliest recognizable manifestation of modern Iñupiaq culture in Alaska). Wales, Alaska is a small village originally known as Kiŋigin and the people who live there refer to themselves as Kingikmiut (the people of Kiŋigin). Kiŋigin and the Wales sites are strategically located at the point where the Russian mainland lies within reach by umiak from North America, about 68 miles. In the past, Kiŋigin was the hub through which people, their material culture, and ideas would have passed from Siberia to Alaska since the submersion of the Bering Land Bridge by the Bering Sea.

Anangula Archeological District National Historic Landmark
Anangula, Alaska

The Anangula Archeological District National Historic Landmark is the earliest known settlement in the Aleutian Islands and was built by ancestors of Unangax̂ (Alaskan Aleut). This landmark is on the tiny island of Ananiuliak (or Anangula Island), which resembles a seal swimming in profile. The archeological district is made up of the Anangula Village site and the Anangula Core and Blade manufacturing site. The Core and Blade site is around 9,000 years old. At the village site there are dozens of ancient house ruins. At Nikolski Village on nearby Umnak Island the residents trace their ancestry back to the Anangula Village site. Unangax̂ people have transferred cultural practices, technology, and artistic style from generation to generation for thousands of years.

SS Nenana National Historic Landmark
Fairbanks, Alaska

The SS Nenana is a wooden-hulled, western rivers-style sternwheel passenger boat. It is one of only three steam-powered passenger sternwheelers of any kind left in the U.S. and the only large wooden sternwheeler. The SS Nenana was built in 1933 for Alaska Railroad service on the Yukon, Nenana, and Tanana Rivers, and the boat provided access to Interior Alaska long before roads could be built. The sternwheeler carried military cargo during World War II, including Lend-Lease aircraft on their way to the Soviet Union. Retired in 1955, Nenana now resides at Pioneer Park in Fairbanks where visitors can see it up close. The SS Nenana represents a period when our nation's rivers were used as major transportation routes.

**Kodiak Naval Operating Base and Forts Greely and Abercrombie
National Historic Landmark
Kodiak, Alaska**

Kodiak Naval Operating Base, with its air station, submarine base, North Pacific Force, and joint operations center for the Navy and Army Air Force, was operational at the time of the Japanese attack on Pearl Harbor in 1941. Kodiak served for a time as the main forward operating base for the defense of Alaska, and for operations and planning to drive the Japanese out from the Aleutians during WWII. U.S. Army Forts Greely and Abercrombie, with their coastal artillery, and infantry troops, stood ready to defend the base. Coordinating with the naval establishments at Sitka and Dutch Harbor, aircraft from the base made vital patrols of the Gulf of Alaska, Bering Sea, and North Pacific Ocean. Ships and submarines also played important roles. Today's U.S. Coast Guard Station Kodiak, operating within the historic installation, provides vital aerial search and rescue in Alaska's vast waters.

Yukon Island Main Site National Historic Landmark
Kachemak Bay, Alaska

Yukon Island is called Ni'ka ("big island") in Athabascan. The Island's position at the outlet of Kachemak Bay is the ideal vantage point to oversee the passage of boats in and out of the bay, and to control access to the bay's wealth of resources. Kachemak Bay and the Gulf of Alaska region are an intersection where Athabascan, Yup'ik, and Alutiiq territories overlap. Archeological sites in Kachemak Bay have been found to extend from 2500 BCE (Before Common Era) to the recent past. The Yukon Island sites were studied by Dr. Frederica de Laguna, the first woman anthropologist and archeologist to dedicate her career to Alaskan history. Dr. de Laguna excavated the Yukon Island sites on her first expedition to Alaska in 1930, bringing her brother Wallace as her assistant and as a bear guard. She wrote the Archaeology of Cook Inlet, Alaska (1934), the first modern monograph on Alaska culture and history about an area little understood by outsiders.

Russian-American Building No. 29 National Historic Landmark
Sitka, Alaska

Building No. 29 was built in 1852 by the Russian-American Company in order to provide living accommodations for Company employees. Its construction was typical for the Russian period with a two-story hewn log structure on a stone foundation, a high attic space, and a high-pitched gable roof with tiled covering and a two-story entrance gallery, or seni, on the east side of the main unit. The main part of the building was nearly square, with all sides measuring approximately four sazhens (28 feet) in length. Changes to the original building include a two-story addition to the east and four evenly spaced dormers along the roof. Today, visitors can view a section of the exterior log wall which displays the original hand-hewn logs, nails, and identification markings.

Holy Assumption Orthodox Church National Historic Landmark
Kenai, Alaska

The Holy Assumption Orthodox Church site consists of the church, rectory (priest residence), chapel, and a cemetery. The church is a fine example of a Russian village church; it is a classic of the Pskov (vessel or ship) design. The rectory is typical of the homes of the Russian village gentry and at the time of its construction was clearly a substantial landmark, being the only two-story structure in the community. The chapel is an excellent example of Russian techniques of log construction, its uncovered log walls an illustration of the excellent craftsmanship and engineering of the Russian-trained builders of the Kenai peninsula. Built in 1895-1896, it is among the oldest standing Orthodox churches in Alaska and retains a high degree of historic integrity to this day.

Fort William H. Seward National Historic Landmark
Haines, Alaska

Fort William H. Seward, built in 1902, was the last of twelve Gold Rush era military posts established in Alaska to control the lawless stampeders. Fort Seward provided the only military presence in the region during boundary disputes with Canada. From 1925 to 1940, the fort was the only active Army installation in Alaska. During World War II it served as a recruitment station, rest stop, and training ground for troops before being decommissioned in 1945. Fort Seward is the best surviving example of a Gold Rush era Alaskan Army fort and the only U.S. military fort associated with Alaska-Canada boundary dispute. It is an outstanding example of an Endicott Era fort in its layout, and architecture. Today, the landmark district has multiple private owners.

Eagle Historic District National Historic Landmark
Eagle, Alaska

Eagle began as a fur trading post around 1880, and by the turn of the 20th century, the fledgling town became the judicial and transportation hub for interior Alaska, with the adjacent Fort Egbert serving as the military and communications center. The rush of gold seekers to Canada's Klondike in the late 1890s brought national attention to Eagle, which was situated in a prime site along the Yukon River, a few miles from the Canadian border. Some miners discovered gold at nearby American Creek and set up camp in Eagle. Fort Egbert was established next to the town in 1899. Today the Bureau of Land Management and Eagle Historical Society and Museums manage some of the historic buildings with exhibits open to the public. Other historic buildings within the National Historic Landmark are privately owned.

Attu Battlefield and U.S. Army and Navy Airfields National Historic Landmark
Attu Island, Alaska

The 12,500 American soldiers landing on Attu Island in May 1943 anticipated needing only a few days to oust the Japanese garrison. Two weeks later, the Americans succeeded after battling the enemy in difficult terrain, harsh weather, and inadequate gear. Occupying Attu and Kiska as part a coordinated attack on the U.S. Pacific Fleet at Midway in June 1942, marked the peak of Japan's military expansion in the Pacific. Attu, the only WWII land battle fought in North America, ranked as the second deadliest battle in the Pacific Theater (in proportion to the number of troops engaged) just behind Iwo Jima. The battle was an important morale booster that demonstrated the worthiness of the American soldier against the enemy as well as illustrating the loyalty of the Japanese soldier to his cause. Lessons learned in amphibious landings, tactics, logistical planning, and Army gear made significant contributions to future U.S. Pacific operations.

Chilkoot Trail and Dyea National Historic Landmark
Skagway, Alaska

The Chilkoot Trail was traditionally used as a trade route between the Tlingit people of Alaska and the Carcross Tagish First Nation people in Canada. As more miners and prospectors came to the area, the Tlingits faced mounting pressure to allow foreigners to use the trail. In 1879, an agreement was reached that would allow miners to use the pass, with the understanding that Tlingit and Tagish packers would be hired to assist. Dyea's real boom began in the fall of 1897 as word spread of the wealth of the Klondike. For months, jammed boatloads of prospectors disembarked in Dyea and streamed north over the Chilkoot Pass. On April 3, 1898, a deadly snow slide near the summit brought worldwide negative publicity and travelers began steering away from Dyea in favor of Skagway. Today, visitors to Klondike Gold Rush National Historical Park can hike the first 33 miles of the trail, witnessing sites and passing by artifacts left behind by gold seekers.

Church of the Holy Ascension National Historic Landmark
Unalaska, Alaska

The Church of the Holy Ascension is located on the Island of Unalaska, approximately halfway along the Aleutian archipelago in the Bering Sea. The site represents Russian missionary activities in the area and is also associated with the career of the first resident Orthodox Bishop of Alaska. The church itself, built in 1894-1896 in the cruciform style, with three altars, is the oldest church of this type in Alaska. Within the nave of the church is an impressive ikonostasis, which is a wall of icons and religious paintings separating the nave from the sanctuary. The church contains a chapel to the north dedicated to St. Innocent of Irkutsk, and one to the south dedicated to St. Sergius. Located to the west is the Bishop's House, which was once part of a larger complex of buildings serving as an orphanage and schoolhouse.

**Dutch Harbor Naval Operating Base and Fort Mears, U.S. Navy National Historic Landmark
Unalaska, Alaska**

World War II came to Alaska when the Japanese bombed the Dutch Harbor Naval Operating and Army bases in early June 1942. Japanese military command had coordinated their attack with one at Midway; followed by invading and occupying Attu and Kiska islands. While the U.S. military scrambled to oust the invaders, during the Aleutian Campaign, a lesser-known impact of the war was the forced evacuation of the Native population. Attu residents were taken to Japan as POWs for the duration of the war. The American forces relocated nearly 900 Alaska Natives from their Aleutian homes to Southeast Alaska where they were relegated to substandard living conditions and suffered other hardships. Today, materials and interviews are available on-line that share their life altering stories, while the landmark maintains much of the strategic defense components of the "Iron Ring" with a lookout post built into the precarious rock cliffs overlooking Unalaska Bay.

Kijik Archeological District National Historic Landmark
Lake Clark, Alaska

The Kijik Archeological District National Historic Landmark, known locally as Qizhjeh, is a collection of village sites that span the past 2,000 years. Residents of current-day Nondalton village are the direct descendants of people who built villages at Kijik (Qizhjeh). The National Historic Landmark is within Lake Clark National Park and Preserve. The houses, steam baths, underground caches, community houses, and Russian Orthodox church that make up the district are the largest concentration of Dena'ina Athabascan sites in Southwest Alaska. This landmark preserves extraordinary opportunities to recognize and study the historic complexities of Athabascan culture.

Cape Nome Mining District and Discovery Sites National Historic Landmark
Nome, Alaska

The discovery of gold at Anvil Creek in 1898 was the first large gold placer strike to be made in Alaska proper. The next year, miners discovered gold in the Nome Beach sand. This discovery created a frenzy, since a miner could not stake a claim on a beach and sand did not require strenuous digging. Many crowded onto the shores of the Bering Sea seeking an easy, quick fortune. As a result, Nome became a booming gold rush town and the focus of Alaska's greatest gold rush, both in gold yield and the increase in population. Gold production reached its peak in 1906. In total, the boom era of 1899 to 1910 yielded over $46 million in gold. The Cape Nome discovery sites represent the culminating episode in the national gold rush phenomenon (Illustration inspired by Eric Hegg photographs, University of Washington Libraries).

Kake Cannery National Historic Landmark
Kake, Alaska

Located in Southeast Alaska, the Kake Cannery began canning operations in 1912. Village residents and local fishermen supplied the cannery with pink and chum salmon, while multi-ethnic laborers helped clean and butcher the catch. In 1949 the Organized Village of Kake, under the Indian Reorganization Act, acquired the cannery in trust through the U.S. Government. At its peak, the cannery was the heartbeat of the community, with virtually all residents a part of it in some fashion. Thanks to stabilization and rehabilitation efforts by tribal staff and other preservation professionals, the cannery buildings can be adapted for new use and facilitate economic development in the Kake area. Historic American Engineering Record documentation illustrates the cannery buildings and their role in the canning process, as well as the fishing methods and technologies developed during the peak of the industry.

**Seal Islands National Historic Landmark
St. George and St. Paul Islands, Alaska**

The Unangax̂ people of the Pribilof islands were instrumental in the commercial harvesting and processing of fur seals for nearly 200 years. When Russian traders discovered the Northern Fur Seal which was the world's largest single herd of mammals, the Pribilof islands became the primary fur seal processing site. This industry generated conflict between nations and peoples from the time of the Russian landing in 1786 until Alaska statehood in 1959. An international conservation agreement signed in 1911 ensured the preservation of the flourishing fur seal herds on the islands of St. Paul and St. George in an important example of the principle of international arbitration. Today, the seals are harvested for subsistence use. Both islands continue to reflect the decades long settlement pattern based on the arrangements of houses, with Russian Orthodox Churches, and other community and commercial buildings present that reflect the unique life and labor force of the early fur seal industry (Illustration, inspired by photograph by Victor B. Scheffer, Courtesy of NOAA NMMI, Library).

**Sitka Naval Operating Base and U.S. Army Coastal Defenses National Historic Landmark
Sitka, Alaska**

The Sitka Naval Operating Base was the Navy's first air station in Alaska, playing a key role in the defense of North America during World War II. When Japan attacked Pearl Harbor in 1941, Sitka had the only major military base in Alaska. Established as an Advanced Seaplane Base in 1937, the base's designation changed several times before becoming the Naval Operating Base in 1942. To provide for defense of the base, the U.S. Army Coastal Defenses were built on the islands west of Japonski Island. After Pearl Harbor, PBY aircraft from Sitka patrolled southeast Alaska and far into the Gulf of Alaska. The Sitka base supported operations throughout most of the war but was decommissioned in 1944 following the successful Aleutian Campaign. Today, many of the WWII structures are used and maintained by multiple owners (Illustration inspired by 1943 photo from the Sitka Historical Society and Museum).

Gallagher Flint Station Archeological Site National Historic Landmark
North Slope, Alaska

Discovered in 1970, during environmental surveys for the construction of the Trans-Alaska Pipeline, the Gallagher Flint Station site was once one of the earliest dated archeological sites in northern Alaska. It demonstrates strong affinities between the indigenous peoples of Alaska and Siberia. The landmark is in the Upper Sagavanirktok River Valley about 250 miles north of the Arctic Circle. It is made up of various stone tool manufacturing debris on top of a prominent kame in the arctic tundra. A kame is a gravel hill left behind by a melting glacier. The landmark's commanding view of the game-rich tundra has lent to its repeated use by hunters over the past 10,000 years. The region is a well-known to big game hunters from Alaska and around the world for its caribou herd.

Use this page for drawing a place important to you!

 Learn more about the National Historic Landmarks in this book
WWW.NPS.GOV/SUBJECTS/NHLALASKA